NO

NOV   2007

EDGE BOOKS™

DRAWING COOL STUFF

HOW TO DRAW

MONSTER TRUCKS

by Aaron Sautter

illustrated by Rod Whigham

Capstone
press

Mankato, Minnesota

Edge Books are published by Capstone Press,
151 Good Counsel Drive, P.O. Box 669, Mankato, Minnesota 56002.
www.capstonepress.com

Library of Congress Cataloging-in-Publication Data
Sautter, Aaron.
How to draw monster trucks / by Aaron Sautter; illustrated by Rod Whigham
p. cm.—(Edge books. Drawing cool stuff)
Includes bibliographical references and index.
Summary; "Lively text and fun illustrations describe how to draw monster
trucks"—Provided by publisher.
ISBN–13: 978-1-4296-0079-8 (hardcover)
ISBN–10: 1-4296-0079-9 (hardcover)
1. Trucks in art—Juvenile literature. 2. Drawing—Technique—Juvenile literature.
I. Whigham, Rod, 1954– II. Title. III. Series.
NC825.T76S28 2008
743'.8962922—dc22   2007003455

Credits
Jason Knudson, designer

1 2 3 4 5 6 12 11 10 09 08 07

TABLE OF CONTENTS

Welcome!

You probably picked this book because you love the car-crushing power of monster trucks. Or maybe you picked it because you like to draw. Whatever the reason, get ready to dive into the world of mighty monster trucks!

The incredible size and power of monster trucks have entertained people for years. They love the roar of huge engines and giant tires that crush cars and rip through thick mud. There are many kinds of monster trucks, but they all have one thing in common—awesome destruction!

This book is just a starting point. Once you've learned how to draw the monster trucks in this book, you can start drawing your own. Let your imagination run wild, and see what kinds of monster truck mayhem you can create!

To get started, you'll need some supplies:

1. First you'll need drawing paper. Any type of blank, unlined paper will do.

2. Pencils are the easiest to use for your drawing projects. Make sure you have plenty of them.

3. You have to keep your pencils sharp to make clean lines. Keep a pencil sharpener close by. You'll use it a lot.

4. As you practice drawing, you'll need a good eraser. Pencil erasers wear out very fast. Get a rubber or kneaded eraser. You'll be glad you did.

5. When your drawing is finished, you can trace over it with a black ink pen or thin felt-tip marker. The dark lines will really make your work stand out.

6. If you decide to color your drawings, colored pencils and markers usually work best. You can also use colored pencils to shade your drawings and make them more lifelike.

Comin' At Ya!

If you see this giant machine coming at you, you'd better run! The driver sits so high that he probably can't see you. Those huge tires would squash you like a bug. Don't ever get in front of a monster truck that's coming your way!

After drawing this truck, try adding your own cool paint designs on the hood.

STEP 1

STEP 2

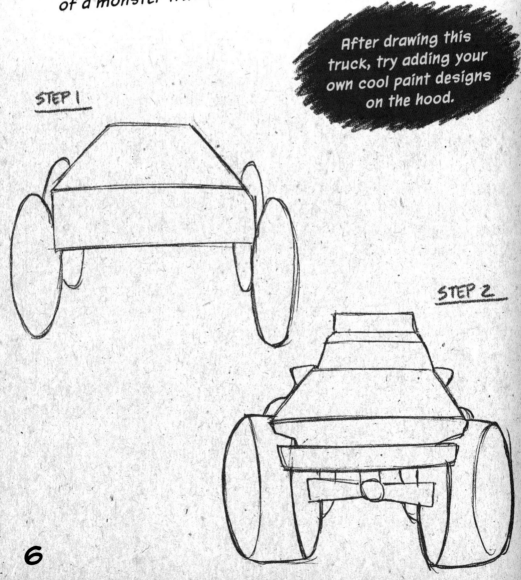

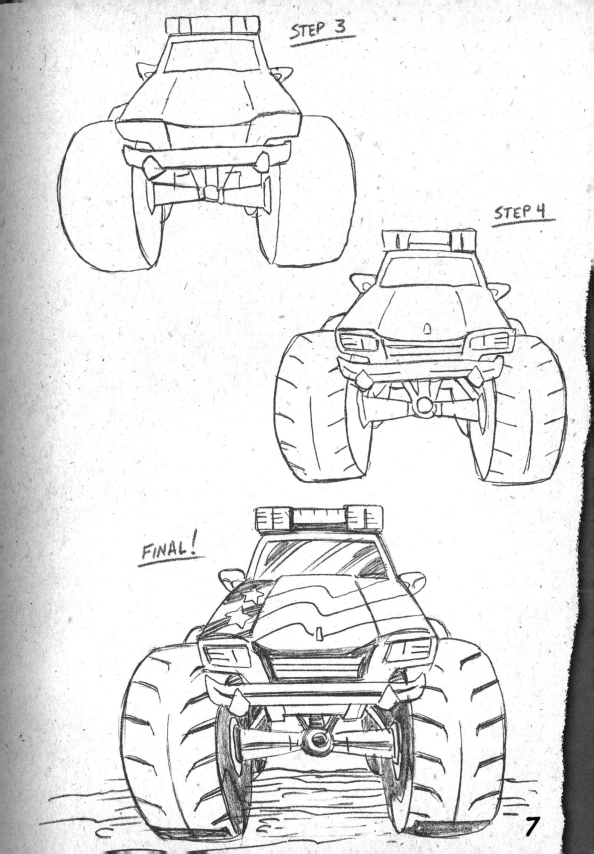

STEP 3

STEP 4

FINAL!

7

TALON

Talon isn't the biggest monster truck. But its sleek, streamlined body and powerful engine make it one of the fastest trucks around. Talon has little competition when it comes to mud racing or distance jumping.

After practicing this drawing, try it again with a bigger engine or even bigger tires!

STEP 1

STEP 2

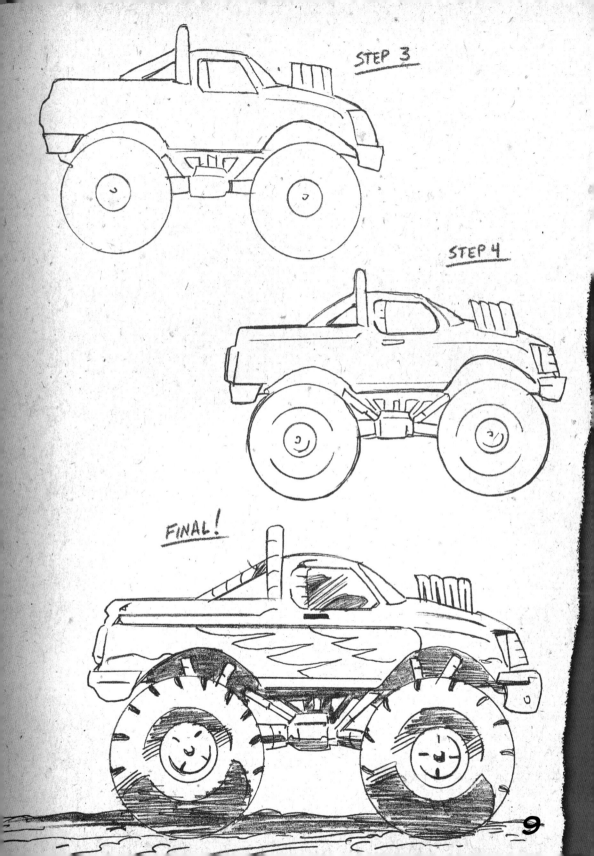

STEP 3

STEP 4

FINAL!

9

DESTRUCTO

Destructo is a master of demolition. This beast smashes cars like they were soda cans. Before each event, Destructo's driver likes to wave to the fans before the destruction begins.

When you're done with this drawing, try giving Destructo some cars to crunch under its wheels!

STEP 1

STEP 2

STEP 3

STEP 4

FINAL!

SKY WARRIOR

When it comes to getting big air, Sky Warrior is the master. This high-flying monster holds many jumping records. Sky Warrior once leaped over 30 cars for a distance of 180 feet. That's more than half a football field!

After drawing this picture, try it again from a distance. See how high you can make Sky Warrior fly!

STEP 1

STEP 2

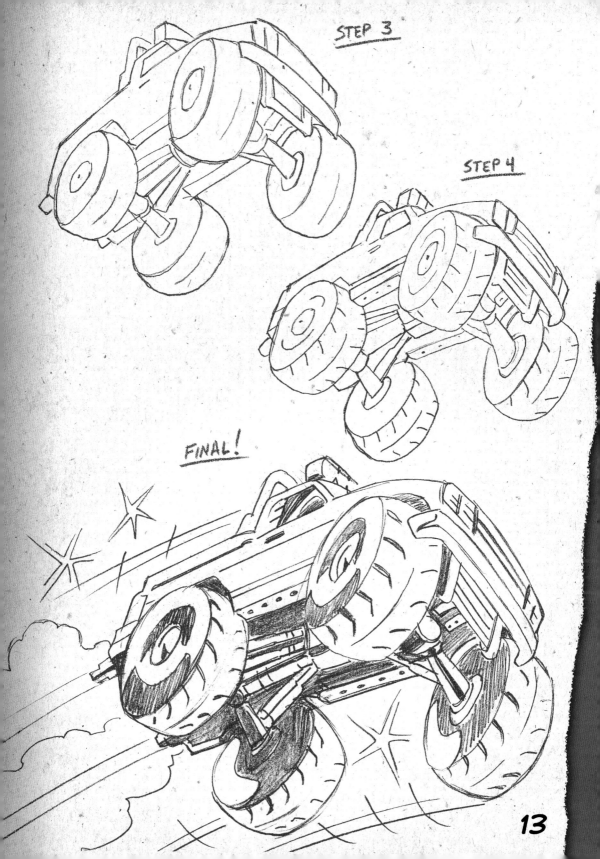

STEP 3

STEP 4

FINAL!

MONSTER CRASH

It's not always high-flying, car-crushing fun at monster truck events. Sometimes drivers push their trucks too hard and they flip over or crash. But watching these huge machines tumble out of control is almost as fun as watching them smash cars to bits.

When you're done with this drawing, try showing the truck on its side or missing some tires!

STEP 1

STEP 2

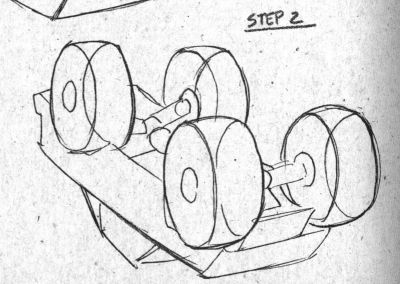

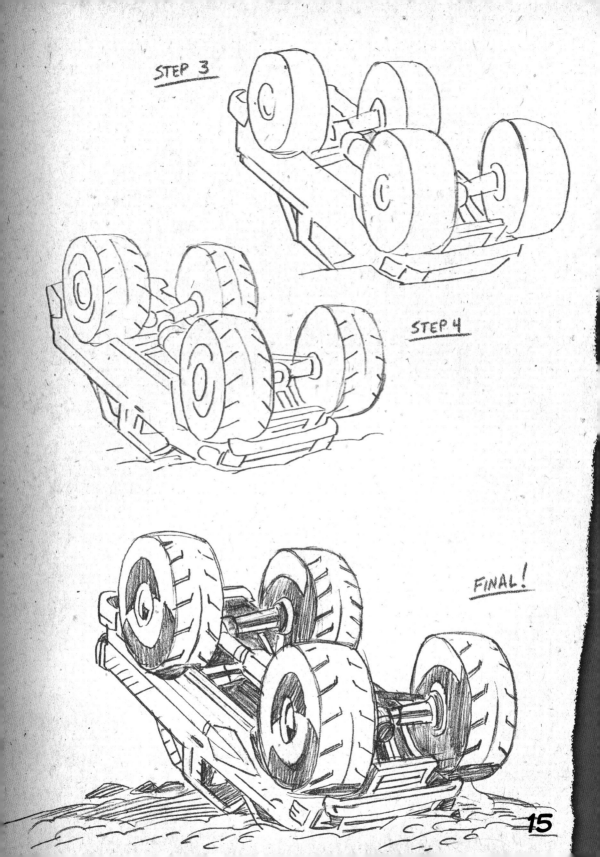

STEP 3

STEP 4

FINAL!

15

SURF 'N TURF

Catch the wave of excitement when Surf 'N Turf hits the track! This monster van gets its name from "surfing" through the air with big jumps and ripping through thick mud. Surf's up, dude!

After practicing this drawing, try out your own cool ideas for a surfing monster truck.

STEP 1

STEP 2

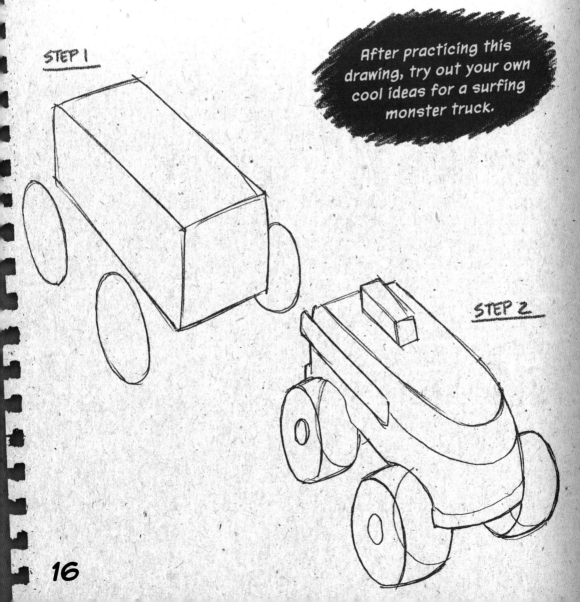

STEP 3

STEP 4

FINAL!

17

BLAZE-OUT

What better way to deal with a monster fire than with a monster fire truck? Blaze-Out makes safety fun at monster truck events. Almost everyone wants to be a firefighter after seeing Blaze-Out in action!

Try showing Blaze-Out putting out a fire. How do you think this truck shoots out water?

STEP 1

STEP 2

STEP 3

STEP 4

FINAL!

FIRE

19

RAGING BULL

Raging Bull easily crunches cars, pickup trucks, and even buses under its massive tires. When it's not tearing up the track, this truck is a champion in weight pulling competitions. You don't want this monster charging after you!

After practicing this drawing, try showing Raging Bull charging through some thick, sticky mud!

STEP 1

STEP 2

STEP 3

STEP 4

FINAL!

21

THE GENERAL

The General is on a mission—of total destruction! Every driver had better pay attention because The General is about to teach them a few new tricks. No other machine can claim the total destructive power The General displays at every event.

When you're done with this drawing, try making your own monster military machine!

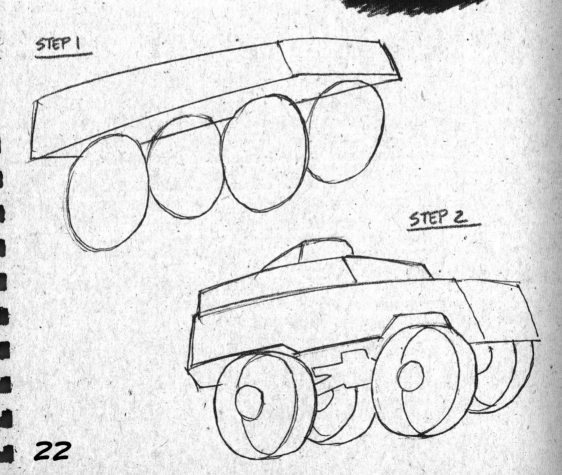

STEP 1

STEP 2

STEP 3

STEP 4

FINAL!

23

KRUSHER KROC

Krusher Kroc is known for dealing out maximum damage. The driver of this overgrown lizard likes ramming other trucks and knocking them out of rallies and races. Most drivers know to stay out of the way of this hulking monster. That's one angry reptile!

After practicing this drawing, try drawing a new fierce creature design of your own!

STEP 1

STEP 2

STEP 3

STEP 4

FINAL!

THUNDER BLAST

Thunder Blast is a major force at every monster truck event. Though it isn't the biggest or most menacing truck around, it has power where it counts. A huge V12 engine and giant tires easily reduce cars to piles of scrap metal.

After you've mastered this drawing, try giving Thunder Blast some even bigger vehicles to crush!

STEP 1

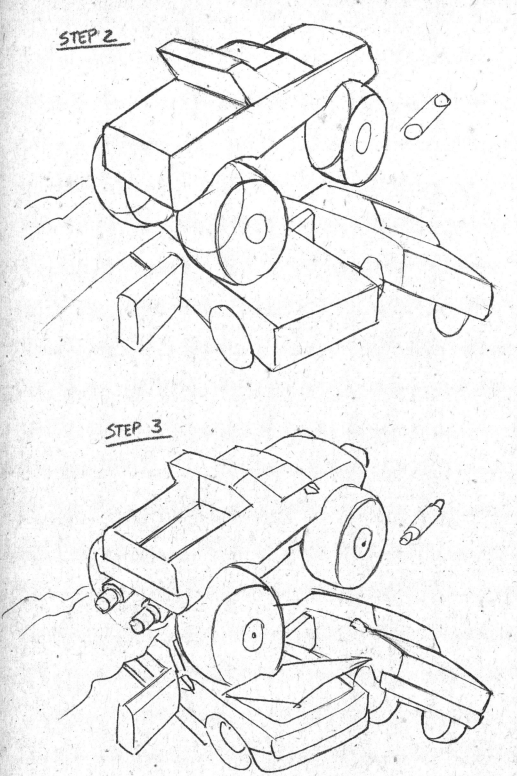

STEP 2

STEP 3

TO FINISH THIS DRAWING,
TURN TO THE NEXT PAGE!

27

STEP 4

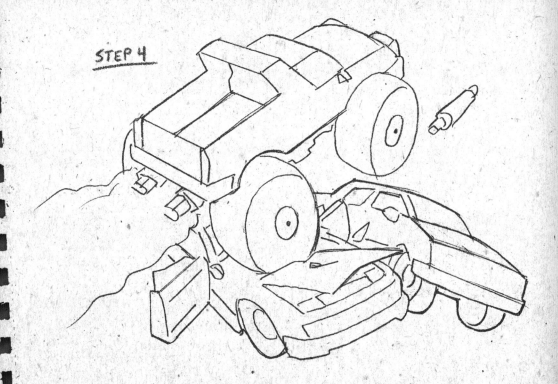

STEP 5

FINAL!

29

GLOSSARY

demolition (dem-uhl-ISH-uhn)—the act of destroying something

design (di-ZINE)—the shape or style of something

destruction (di-STRUHK-shuhn)—what happens when something is destroyed

rally (RAL-ee)—a large gathering of people with similar interests; races and other competitions often happen at rally events.

reptile (REP-tile)—a cold-blooded animal with a backbone

streamlined (STREEM-lined)—designed to move easily and quickly through air or water

surfing (SURF-ing)—using a board to ride on waves

READ MORE

Barr, Steve. *1-2-3 Draw Cartoon Trucks and Motorcycles: A Step-by-Step Guide.* 1-2-3 Draw. Columbus, N.C.: Peel Productions, 2005.

Muehlenhardt, Amy Bailey. *Drawing and Learning About Monster Trucks: Using Shapes and Lines.* Sketch It! Minneapolis: Picture Window Books, 2006.

Teitelbaum, Michael, and Ron Zalme. *How to Draw Monster Jam.* New York: Scholastic, 2003.

INTERNET SITES

FactHound offers a safe, fun way to find Internet sites related to this book. All of the sites on FactHound have been researched by our staff.

Here's how:
1. Visit *www.facthound.com*
2. Choose your grade level.
3. Type in this book ID code **1429600799** for age-appropriate sites. You may also browse subjects by clicking on letters, or by clicking on pictures and words.
4. Click on the **Fetch It** button.

FactHound will fetch the best sites for you!

INDEX